Copyright © 2020 by Phillips Coleman Ph.d

All rights reserved. No part of this publication may be reproduced, distributed, or transmitted in any form or by any means, including photocopying, recording, or other electronic or mechanical methods, without the prior written permission of the publisher, except in the case of brief quotation embodied in critical reviews and certian other noncommercial uses permitted by copyright law.

Table of Contents

Introductions 3
What is Gardening? 6
gardening tools 9
what is succulents plants? 49
    Types of succulents of plant 51
Types of Succulent Gardening 70
How to Plant a Succulent Garden 80
    How to Plant a Succulent 83
Tip of succulents Gardening 85
Advantages of Succulent gardening 92
Disadvantages of Succulent Gardening 108
conclusion 115

Introductions

Unique for their ability to store water, succulents are well suited for climates with high temperatures and low rainfall. Many people think of them as desert plants, but they also thrive in coastal locales. Gardeners love them for their drought resistance, architectural forms, vivid colors and ease of maintenance. Succulents are especially popular for use in containers. Whether you need a groundcover or a specimen plant, there is a succulent for every situation. Some form small rosettes, some trail up to 3 feet, while still others grow to resemble small trees. When healthy, many will produce pups or eye-catching blooms. Additionally, they work well in a variety of garden styles including modern, Mediterranean, tropical, rock gardens, xeriscapes and more. This section is filled with ideas for growing succulents in your own garden. Browse the articles and images to see how top designers incorporate these plants into their gardens.succulent gardens are among the easiest ways to enjoy wonderfully diverse plants in difficult, dry sites, on small patios, and indoors. Learning to make a succulent garden can become a cool hobby that won't require a lot of time or maintenance. Garden succulents are fleshy plants that store water in leaves and stems, and provide a fascinating assortment of shapes, sizes, and colors, and often have unique frills, spines, and beautiful flowers. Succulents can be native to arid deserts, cold mountainsides, or steamy jungle. Some will freeze easily, while some are cold hardy to well below zero, even in the harsh winters of our northern states. Commonly-grown succulent garden plants include many unique species of Agave, Crassula, Sedum, Euphorbia, Kalanchoe, Sansevieria, Aloe, Sempervivum, Yucca, and more.

What is Gardening?

Gardening, the laying out and care of a plot of ground devoted partially or wholly to the growing of plants such as flowers, herbs, or vegetables. Gardening can be considered both as an art, concerned with arranging plants harmoniously in their surroundings, and as a science, encompassing the principles and techniques of plant cultivation. Because plants are often grown in conditions markedly different from those of their natural environment, it is necessary to apply to their cultivation techniques derived from plant physiology, chemistry, and botany, modified by the experience of the planter. The basic principles involved in growing plants are the same in all parts of the world, but the practice naturally needs much adaptation to local conditions.

gardening tools

Weeder

If you want to tackle weeds, but you don't want to pollute your garden with harmful chemicals the best solution is a simple weeder. These are small hand tools with a forked end that's ideal for digging individual weeds and removing them by the root. If used correctly you can remove all of the offending plant so that it doesn't come back to haunt you! Be ready for some hard work though –

removing weeds one at a time is a time consuming process. On the bright side you'll get to spend quality time outdoors, soaking up that valuable vitamin D! The Vremi Garden Weeder is a really sturdy, comfortable to use weeding tool. It's great for loosening and pulling up those long, hard to reach dandelion roots!

Garden Scissors

Scissors are an essential, but often overlooked tool for any real gardener. The reason is simple –

they're a highly versatile piece of equipment that can be used to do a lot of simple chores. You can use them for opening seed packets, for delicate pruning jobs of small flowers, and at a pinch, you can even use them for digging out weeds if nothing else is available. (Just make sure you clean them thoroughly afterwards!) A gardener has to be ready to improvise when the right tool is not at hand – with a little imagination you can accomplish anything in the garden with very few tools. The Very Sharp Multi-Purpose Scissors by RiverView

Enterprise, with their reinforced blades, are suitable for both left and right Handed people to use. A no-nonsense, durable pair of scissors for the garden at an excellent price.

Soil Knife

A soil knife is another versatile tool, but surprisingly not one that the average gardener has in his/her tool box. These tools are of Japanese origin and are sometimes referred to as a Hori-Hori.

They're ideal for all kinds of jobs that involve digging and cutting. However, the serrated blade is usually sharp on both ends and at the point, so it's probably a good idea to keep it out of reach of small children.

soil knife

If this is the first time you've ever heard of one of these then you may want to head out to the local hardware store and pick one up – you'll be glad that you did.

Digging Knife, is made from high quality stainless steel, features a full width, bend-resistant tang with a concave blade for easy digging. It has a serrated side and a sharp side which makes it a versatile and very useful garden tool. It comes in a strong leather sheath.

Hand Trowel

Our garden needed a lot of work as the previous owners weren't exactly green fingered!

You can use a trowel for digging out areas for plants and flowers as well as refilling the holes when you're finished. They're also ideal for digging out any weeds that have encroached on your garden plots. I've even used one for a little edging work from time to time – there may be more specialized tools for this, but they'll do at a pinch.

The True Temper Hand Transplanter Trowel is a well-made, nice sharp pointed trowel for transplanting work that requires precision cutting and digging.

The Fiskars Big Grip Trowel is an extremely durable, cast aluminum trowel which will stand up to heavy duty handling, unlike many other trowels which often break at the weak spot between the handle and shovel end. By contrast, this Fiskars trowel is extremely robust and won't let you down.

Pruning Shears

We have a beautiful Chinese Cherry tree in our front yard, but every spring it's an unholy mess to behold. After a winter of very little attention, the branches have a habit of sprouting all over the place. That's why I always make sure I have a good pair of pruning shears in the garage ready for action.

They have to be sharp though if you're going to use them on small trees. It's a good idea to sharpen them every spring so that you're not frustrated by trying to prune with a dull pair of shears.

garden pruning shears

The FELCO 2 Pruning Shears are great for most gardeners. You really can't go wrong with these professional quality, classic pruning shears which have been proven time and again by horticulturists and farmers the world over.

A Good Old Water Hose or Sprinkling System

Once you've finished laying out your garden, it's a great feeling when you can stand back and admire the finished article – but that doesn't mean you're done for the rest of the year! Keeping a garden looking nice and just the way you want it requires regular maintenance.

Other than sunshine, what's the one thing that flowers and plants simply must have? Why water of course! That's why a good quality hose for your garden is indispensable – and while you're at it, you might also wish to consider a sprinkler system.

Expandable Garden Hose is both durable and lightweight, has solid brass fittings so it won't rust, and comes with all the attachments you need including the spray gun.

The easy to set up Lawn Sprinkler by Wshan gives great coverage (adjustable spray up to 16 feet) and comes with a hose attachment as well as a rotary butterfly sprinkler.

Curved Blade Digging Shovel

A full length curved blade digging shovel is a staple gardening tool in most garden sheds and for good reason – if you want a beautiful garden it's a must have.

You can use a full length curved shovel for many heavy duty digging jobs including planting trees and large shrubs. They're also great for working over a lot of soil in a short period of time.

In the early spring I typically use mine to loosen up the soil to get it ready for planting before using the rake to break down the lumps and get the soil into that fine, smooth finish ready for planting.

Full Flat Digging Shovel / Spade

A round shovel isn't the only shovel you should have in your garden shed though. They do have their limitations. Specifically, they're not great for edging work.

If you're trying to move a section of grass to make a new garden plot, a curved shovel will only get you so far. Once you've dug out your plot it's time to trim the edges and for that you need a full length flat shovel.

With a flat straight edge you can finish plotting out the perfect garden section and make your yard look exactly how you'd envisioned it.

Steel Digging Spade is a rugged, well-balanced spade which you will be proud to own. It has a mirror polished, sharp stainless steel head for maximum rust resistance and minimal soil adhesion.

The one-piece weather-proof, hardwood shaft is split to form a wishbone handle and will prove its worth time and again.

Leaf Rakes

Anyone that spends a lot of time in the garden likes to rake up all the leaves up in the fall and then again in spring – along with any other debris that's built up over the winter months.

The best tool for this job is a leaf rake with a large fan like blade. The bristles are typically made from a soft flexible metal or plastic material that allows you to lightly rake the whole surface of all the debris, but still leaves the soil in place.

It's one of the first garden tools I ever used as a kid when it was my job to rake the leaves – I had to earn my allowance somehow!

leaf rake

The all-singing, all dancing Gonicc 63-Inch Professional Adjustable Garden Leaf Rake, is a welcome and truly innovatory product. It has a telescopic handle, which means that whatever height you are, you can adjust it to suit.

Additionally the rake head can be adjusted from a 7-inch rake to 22 inches simply by opening the easy to use locking lever. This makes it extremely versatile for getting into all the corners as well as opened out wide for use on the lawn.

Garden Rakes

Leaf rakes are invaluable, but they're horribly frustrating if you're trying to use them as a finishing tool on your soil. For that you need something a little more rigid and that's where a garden rake which is specifically made for cultivation, comes in.

If you're not familiar with these they have a solid flat blade set at an angle at the end of a long pole with several solid "tines" sticking out from the edge of the blade.

Their rigid nature makes it much easier to break down the surface of the soil and give it that nice, neat raked over and well cared-for look.

The traditional Bully Tools 12-Gauge 16-Inch Bow Rake with Fiberglass Handle has a business end made from extra thick 10 gauge steel. It has 16 steel tines and the handle is a high-strength, triple layered fiberglass handle with a wooden core. A solid, well built rake which will last a lifetime.

Pruning Saw

You would normally associate a saw with cutting wood for various woodworking projects, but a good-quality hand pruning saw is also a tool that every gardener should have.

Pruning shears might be great for plants and small branches on trees, but larger branches require something with a little more cutting power. A pruning saw is perfect for this because it designed to cut on the pull stroke, which gives you greater control when sawing branches.

hand pruning saw

Sure you could go with a small chainsaw, but they can be expensive and are really not necessary for 99 percent of all gardening jobs.

The Silky 270-33 Series Curved Blade Hand Saw with Scabbard, is a professional quality Japanese pruning saw with a 13-inch curved, hard chromium blade.

The blade has a full tang, (the part of the blade which goes into the moulded rubber handle), which makes it very stable in use. These Silky saws can either be used by hand or mounted on a Zubat

Professional pole, which adds greatly to its usefulness.

This is one of the sharpest pruning saws you can buy and great care is advised when handling it. It cuts with a pull action and comes with a tailor-made rugged polypropylene, scabbard.

Garden Hoe

In medieval Europe working with the earth was backbreaking work because they didn't have the benefit of modern technology. One thing they did have which made their lives easier, was a primitive version of our garden hoe.

This simple innovation made the job of planting seeds a whole lot easier and while our modern garden hoes may be made from modern materials and designed to last a long time they are essentially the same tool.

They allow you to quickly dig a shallow trench in the soil that's ideal for planting seeds just below the surface. If you're planning on having a vegetable garden a good garden hoe is essential.

Handheld Long Handle Stainless Steel Garden Draw Hoe features a 6-inch stainless steel blade is rust resistant and has a polished wood handle which is durable and easy to grip. Perfect for tasks such as shaping soil, removing weeds, clearing soil of old crops and harvesting rooted vegetables.

The shank is forged in one piece with the blade. This ensures an extremely durable, bend resistant hoe with lots of levering power.

Gardening Gloves

Some people love the feel of the dirt in their hands – it just kind of makes you feel alive. I'm one of those people and if you are too, you might be thinking "what the heck do I need gardening gloves for?"

Even those of us who don't mind getting our hands dirty still need a good pair of gardening gloves. Digging in the dirt with a hand shovel may not seem like the hardest chore, but after a few hours of it your hands will start to feel it. If you want to avoid unwanted blisters a pair of gardening gloves is something you should seriously consider.

Gardening Gloves

These great Garden Gloves for Women and Men have puncture-resistant coating, 3 times thicker than normal ones which reduces cuts and scratches while providing excellent grip and bare-hand sensitivity.

They are made from breathable fabric. The perfect choice for weeding, planting, digging, landscaping, picking fruit, flowers, or vegetables. Machine washable, these gloves come in small medium and large sizes – so they will fit your hand – like a glove!

A Wheelbarrow

When you're digging out new gardens or taking care of a weed infestation you're bound to have a lot of waste material. All of that has to go somewhere and even if you have a backyard compost heap you still have to get it there.

Unless your idea of fun is carrying each individual shovelful of debris over to the compost heap, then a wheelbarrow should be in that garden shed of yours.

You can save a lot of time and effort with a good quality wheelbarrow – just make sure those tyres are properly inflated before you get to work!

The Best Choice Products Dual Wheel Home Wheelbarrow is constructed from powder coated steel, polyurethane, and rubber for a rust proof performance.

The thick padded loop handles double as a stand and make pushing the wheelbarrow comfortable and easy to lift. The dual 13-inch rubber wheels are sturdy and pneumatic, making it easy to manoeuvre over various types of ground. The deep barrow provides an ample 5 cubic feet of space.

A Small Stool

Before I talk about the next item on our list it's probably important to define what we mean by a tool. In our humble opinion a tool is anything that makes your life a little easier and makes it possible to perform a task with less effort than would otherwise be necessary.

That's why a small stool makes our list of essential gardening tool. If you really love gardening and plan on spending several hours a week working on your yard you'll be glad you invested in a small garden stool. They save you from a lot of joint pain and they're definitely a lot easier on your knees.

The Abco Garden Kneeler & Seat makes it easy to kneel in the garden without hurting your knees or back. It comes with a soft foam padding to provide a welcome cushion for your knees – it also helps protect the knees of your pants!

The strong metallic frame provides support for hands and back when kneeling down and standing up. This kneeler can be flipped over to convert it into a comfortable seat when needing a break and it can be folded flat for compact storage.

Knee Pads

If a stool's just not your thing, but you still want to save your knees then you may want to consider a good pair of knee pads. Kneeling down to dig in the garden will take it's toll on your kneecaps over time. If you just can't stand the pain in your knees any longer it's definitely time for a pair of knee pads.

Pads protect your knees against cuts or scrapes on any terrain. They have a soft gel core and durable foam padding to cushion and give great comfort when kneeling.

These quality knee pads are designed to work with the natural hinge action of the knee and have adjustable velcro straps to make sure they stay in place and don't slip down when in use.

Leaf Blower

There are a couple of different ways to get rid of the leaves in your yard and it really comes down to personal preference. I've always used a rake and I'm perfectly happy with my choice.

Some people think this is just a little bit too time consuming though and my father definitely falls into this category. For him, his leaf blower is the best invention since the toaster and there are a lot of people that share that opinion.

It certainly makes short work of blowing the leaves into a corner where at the flick of a switch it then sucks them all up into the bag, ready for emptying on the compost heap.

The Black+Decker BV6000 High Performance Blower, Vac and Mulcher has 2 speed selections and comes complete with its own disposable leaf bag system. This top-quality electric leaf blower is ideal for clearing driveways, sidewalks, decks, and garages of debris and fall leaves from the yard.

Easily switches from blower to vacuum mode, the heavy-duty vacuum eats up leaves, grass clippings, twigs, pine needles, and other lawn debris. The mulch mechanism is excellent – it allows you to grind up to 16 bags of mulch down to one.

Weed Trimmer / Brush Cutter

There is an easier way to get rid of weeds than using a manual weeder like the one we've already mentioned in this article. You can always go with a good-quality weed trimmer – or a strimmer as it's sometimes called and I do have one in my shed as well. I prefer to use mine for larger more daunting tasks, but it is a great option if you're pressed for time.

A brush cutter is a heavier duty version for keeping on top of rougher areas. For more information, check out our guide to the best brush cutters on the market.

The main drawback with these machines is that they don't cut off the roots of the weeds, so they will grow back. I use both a weed trimmer and manual weeder depending on the job and my mood.

The Greenworks 21212 Corded String Trimmer features a simple to maintain design with a 13-inch cutting path. It has an automatic dual line feed, adjustable telescoping shaft and a 180 degree rotating handle for easy edging and trimming. (Don't forget, you'll need to use an extension cable with this trimmer).

Lawn Mower

It may seem obvious, but no garden is going to look to good if you don't look after the lawn. That's why every garden shed simply has to have a good lawn mower in it. Some prefer gas mowers, some electric, and others still prefer the manual push mowers, but whatever your choice you need a mower.

The size of your garden is often the deciding factor – if you have a large garden you'll be glad of the freedom a gas lawn mower gives you but if you only have a small patch to look after then an electric lawnmower may be all you need. Push mowers are fine on the flat but uphill? Mmmm! Not so sure that would work!

This top-rated electric mower has a 5 position height adjustment which allows for the perfect height of cut on all types of grass. It also comes with a 150 feet extension cord.

A Digging Fork

If you need to break up the soil a standard garden rake is okay, but a digging fork is better if you want to get real penetration. You can really get some depth with one of these.

materials like soil, compost or mulch easier than ever.

The welded steel construction is far more durable than wood and won't flex like fiberglass. The angled D-handle keeps your wrist in a neutral position to reduce strain, and pointed boron steel tines make penetrating hard soil easy.

The mid grip, teardrop-shaped shaft provide exceptional comfort and control. The powder-coated steel resists rust and offers easy cleaning and a hang hole allows for convenient storage in your shed or garage.

what is succulents plants?

The meaning of succulent as it relates to food is juicy or tender. The definition of succulent plants is similar: plants that store water in leaves, stems, or both. There are many different types, species, and cultivars of them all, in a fascinating assortment of shapes, sizes, colors, and unique features ranging from frills to spines and beautiful flowers.

To define succulents further, cacti are succulents, but not all succulents are cacti. They can be native to arid deserts, seaside cliffs, cold mountains, or even steamy jungles. Many will simply melt into mush if exposed to freezing temperatures, but there are quite a few which will grow outside during harsh freezing weather, as far north as Canada.

Succulent means that the plants can tolerate prolonged drought, sometimes for months; most grow best in bright light, but not always full hot sun.

Types of succulents of plant

AGAVE

Agaves are available in a wide range of sizes, from smaller specimens that mature at 1-2 feet, perfect for containers, to larger specimens many feet tall and wide. Their fleshy and fibrous leaves grow in a rosette shape and are usually barbed along the edges and tipped with a sharp point, with the exception of Agave attenuata (shown). They come in shades of gray and green, some with hints of blue and red, as well as others that are variegated with white or yellow, such as Agave americana. Most agaves are sun-lovers, but some can survive temperatures as low as the 20s. These sculptural succulents add an impressive design element to your water-wise garden or patio container.

SNAKE PLANT

Commonly called mother-in-law's tongue or snake plant, there are approximately 70 species of Sansevieria. These nearly indestructible plants are often grown indoors and thrive on warmth and bright light, but some also tolerate low light & humidity. The dense, stiff leaves of some types can reach up to 3' tall. Leaves are dark green with grey-green cross banding (Sanseveiria harwoodii) with white or cream variegation on the leaf margins (Sansevieria trifasciata 'Laurentii'), or have cylindrical stems (Sansevieria cylindrica). Sansevieria are well-known for their air-purifying qualities.

ALOE

Aloe plants range in size from just a few inches to tree-varieties up to 20 feet tall. Their gel-filled leaves grow in a rosette pattern, some with marginal teeth, Aloe teeth are not as sharp as the terminal barbs of Agave. Aloes will bloom each year by shooting up tall flower stalks, usually in shades of bright orange, red, or yellow, most commonly mid-winter to summer. Aloes are frost-tender, making smaller, container-size varieties more suitable for moving indoors in colder climates.

YUCCA

With several varieties available, there are yuccas suitable for almost any climate, some being cold hardy well below freezing. Their leaves are stiff and linear, ending in a spear-like spike. Yuccas are quite easy to grow, sometimes too easy, and may have a tendency to offset beyond the original solitary rosette. Species range from tall-stemmed trees topped by a cluster of spikey leaves to stemless varieties 1-2 feet tall and wide. Yucca elephantipes (shown) is a giant, spineless yucca that can be grown in the ground or containers.

PRICKLY PEAR CACTUS

All cacti are considered succulents, and one of the most common is the prickly pear (Opuntia). It is characterized by its flat, fleshy pads that have large spines and smaller, hair-like prickles that easily detach, as experienced by anyone who has come in contact with one. Prickly pears are extremely drought tolerant and also produce showy flowers and edible fruit, making them a perfect dramatic accent for xeriscape planting.

JADE PLANT

Crassula ovata, more commonly known as jade plant, has thick, shiny leaves in shades of green and grey, some with red or yellow edges. Jade is commonly grown as an indoor plant, but can also be grown outdoors in mild climates.

Mature plants will bloom clusters of small pink or white, but will rarely bloom if grown indoors.

KALANCHOE

Kalanchoes are recognized as the most commercially sold succulent. Kalanchoe blossfeldiana (shown) can be readily found in supermarkets, home improvement centers and nurseries, being sold as a houseplant. However, it can also be grown outside in milder climates. Most grow no larger than a couple of feet tall and are well-suited for patio pots or indoor containers. They bloom with long-lasting bright flowers from fall to winter and their textured foliage adds to the show.

STONECROP

Sedum and Hylotelephium are commonly referred to as stonecrops, smaller varieties do well in sunny crevices in stone walls and in sandy areas. They have small, showy flowers that bloom in many colors, abundantly in some species. Some varieties are better suited to cooler weather, preferring milder summers and surviving temperatures below freezing, while others tolerate heat better than cold.

SEMPERVIVUM

Often referred to as hen and chicks, there are over 3000 cultivars of Sempervivum. Like some varieties of Sedum, these also do well in colder climates and are not well-suited for hot, southwest summers. Although they resemble Echeveria, they are more compact and have thinner leaves. Sempervivum are easy to care for and will produce multiple offsets to form a thick mat of foliage. They also thrive in rock gardens or amongst stones or gravel.

ICE PLANT

Delosperma cooperi (shown) is a hardy variety of ice plant native to

South Africa. These spreading ground covers are drought and heat tolerant, and get their name from several varieties that produce calcium crystals on their leaves that resemble frost. Species and cultivars come in a multitude of colors and will provide a showy carpet of vibrant blooms throughout the summer. This ground cover only asks for well-drained soil and bright light.

ECHEVERIA

The many varieties, colors, shapes and sizes of Echeveria make it hard to pick a favorite. Most are rosettes and come in colors ranging from pastels to deeper shades of pink, blue, orange, green and even in combinations. Leaf textures can vary from smooth to bumpy, powdery, or fuzzy. They range in size from 1-2 inches to nearly a foot in diameter. They bloom on tall flower stalks and a common favorite is Echeveria elegans (shown).

EUPHORBIA

This huge genus contains over 2000 species (including poinsettias), with 500 of those being succulents. The common factor is a milky sap that can be irritating to the skin in some varieties and poisonous in others. Some species closely resemble cactus and store water just as efficiently. Some will bloom with tiny flowers. They vary greatly in size from 1-2 inches to trees of 30 feet. Euphorbia tirucalli 'Sticks on Fire' (red pencil tree) shown here is a common variety that can grow to 5 feet tall and wide.

AEONIUM

The symmetrical rosettes that form at the end of the branch-like stems bear resemblance to other succulents such as Echeveria and Sempervivum. The dark magenta-black rosettes of Aeonium arboreum 'Zwartkop'(shown) are actually leaves. Flowers will bloom from the center of the rosette in clusters in late winter or spring. Yellow, green, red or variegated white leaves are also seen in Aeonium.

HAWORTHIA

Haworthia's small size makes it perfect for window boxes. They sunburn easily, so should be protected from direct bright light. They will multiply and tend to establish tight overlapping colonies. Bloom stalks will form and shoot up from the center of the plant, but can be removed if unappealing. Haworthia fasciata (shown) is a favorite for use in mixed succulent plantings.

SENECIO

Senecio mandraliscae, commonly called blue chalksticks (shown), is a groundcover succulent that will form drifts of blue in your landscape. Most types of Senecio will tolerate some frost. There are over 1000 species, but only about 100 that are succulents. These succulent Senecio are drought and heat tolerant.

Types of Succulent Gardening

Rule of Three

It's an investment to obtain several of the same or similar containers, but echoing shapes and colors invariably enhances outdoor living areas. And when grouped, such pots create a focal point. The simple lines and neutral, gunmetal-gray color of this trio by Holloway display the succulents they contain without upstaging them. In two are hens and chicks, which will overwinter outdoors in Vancouver. The middle pot is replanted annually; it showcases green and variegated Aeonium cultivars, blue Senecio mandraliscae, Crassula, and Sedum. Succulents benefit from warmth radiated from the hardscape, and don't drop much leaf litter—a good thing, because these are poolside pots.

Urban Urn

Although another designer might have snapped off the heads of this leggy Aeonium 'Zwartkop' (syn. Aeonium 'Schwarzkopf') and replanted them as cuttings, Holloway used it to lend height to a composition in a client's matte black, concrete, Frank Lloyd Wright-designed urn. Filler plants include: strappy-leaved Yucca aloifolia 'Purpurea', Sedum morganianum, purple-variegated Echeveria nodulosa, blue Senecio serpens, bright-yellow Sedum makinoi 'Ogon', Echeveria 'Powder Blue', and Euphorbia tirucalli 'Sticks on Fire'. When designing with black Aeonium, think of them as silhouettes and position them against a blank wall. If the background is too busy, their dark color makes them disappear.

Succulent Cascade

When Peter Loyola acquired his outdoor café's alley-like space, he saw it not as a characterless rectangle below a looming two-story wall, but rather a canvas awaiting three-dimensional works of living art. He decided to subdue the wall's "screaming red brick" with trailing Senecio radicans (fish hooks) planted in a window box along with Aeonium rosettes. The green of the succulents contrasts with the bricks, and the multiple strands of the Senecio suggest a waterfall. Evidently it loves this location: "In 10 months, I had to trim it four times," Loyola says. "If you're looking for length, fish hooks is the perfect choice."

Closet Door Redux

Loyola enjoys the challenge of planting succulents in architectural salvage. To create containers for plants in the hollowed-out center section of an old door, he cut plastic rain gutters to fit. After drilling drainage holes, he painted the gutters butter yellow, which disguises their original function while giving them prominence and making them integral to the composition. Small rosette succulents tucked into the troughs include Aeonium, Sedum, and Echeveria. Growing in 2 to 3 inches of soil is adequate, he says, and "helps them stay small." He lightly spray-painted the shutters moss green and then sanded to lend a finishing touch.

Driftwood Design

For this 34-by-62-inch vertical garden, Loyola painted a wooden frame pale green, then sanded it to reveal its imperfections. He lined it with a 2-inch-thick sandwich of potting soil and burlap, held in place (front and back) with 18-gauge chicken wire. Driftwood both enhances the design and helps keep the soil from slumping. Using a pointed chopstick to make holes in the burlap, Loyola planted the arrangement (laid flat) with cuttings of Echeveria, Sempervivum, Aeonium, small Crassula, Graptopetalum, and Sedum (notably burro tail). A few weeks later, when roots had anchored the plants, he positioned the planted frame upright.

Echeveria Aloft

For a hard-to-water window box, Holloway chose tall, tapered terracotta pots. "Their height was right and their rolled rims repeat the iron curves," he says. He promised the homeowner that succulents would "spark the interest of passersby" as much or more than petunias or geraniums, with significantly less hassle. (Succulents need infrequent irrigation and seldom require deadheading.) Holloway chose those that resemble flowers—rosette Echeveria in blue, pink, and green—plus Sedum rubrotinctum (pork and beans) for contrast and as a trailer. When sunlit, dramatic lime-green Echeveria pallida glows, enhancing the view from indoors.

Dish Gardens

Holloway says he designed these "hover dish planters" expressly for succulents: "There are hanging baskets; why not hanging dishes?" Succulents, he adds, are shallow-rooted, so shallow containers make sense. He planted these with a mix of small Crassula, Sedum, Sempervivum, and Aeonium. Senecio rowleyanus (string-of-pearls), fish hooks, and Sedum 'Angelina' cascade from the get-go, and other succulents will become pendant over time. In the red dish, adding height and color, are Euphorbia trigona f. rubra and Euphorbia tirucalli 'Sticks on Fire'. Holloway's hover dish planters also look good empty, especially in threes, and could even serve as bird feeders.

How to Plant a Succulent Garden

Succulent gardening involves not only choosing the right plants for your site, but also making sure they get bright light and that their roots don't stay wet for very long - the plants have the ability to tolerate prolonged drought, sometimes going for months without rain in their native lands, and will rot if kept too wet.

A DIY succulent garden is not hard to get started. Many are grown in small or shallow containers, or in raised beds or hillsides, and in succulent rock gardens. In xeric (dry) climates, they are often used in foundation plantings and shrub beds, and even as lawn substitutes.

First, select a garden spot or window that gets a few hours of direct sun; with few exceptions such as Sansevieria, most succulents get leggy and weak if not given bright light, and will develop better foliage color with a direct sun. However, many will scorch when exposed to more than a few hours of hot summer sun, particularly in humid climates. Provide shade from mid-day sun, or a sheer curtain if grown in a south- or west-facing window.

Shallow-rooted succulents can grow perfectly well for many years in small well-drained areas, terraced hillsides, or shallow containers. Next, add coarse sand or grit to your native soil, at least six or eight inches deep to provide drainage during heavy rains. For container gardens, choose a cactus mix or make your own well-drained soil using organic matter such as peat moss or compost plus coarse sand and either crunchy perlite or garden grit.

How to Plant a Succulent

Plant succulents carefully, with soil covering their roots and firm enough with your hand to support the lower stems of larger plants. Don't be tempted to crowd them - depending on the type, give them room to grow taller or to spread. Allow them to settle in for a day or two before watering, to allow broken roots to heal. And avoid watering succulents in mid-day sun.

If possible, protect from hot sun for a week or two. And though a lot of succulents grow best when soil is moist, none want to be kept wet; in general, water often enough to keep plants from shriveling.

Tip of succulents Gardening

Failing to Give Them Enough Light

The natural light of a plant's native habitat is perhaps the most difficult environmental variable to emulate indoors. For common houseplants, we have an easier time. Many are native to tropical jungles and accustomed to the shifting periods of shade and sun that happen in your home. After all, that's what naturally happens as the sun moves over a forest canopy.

But if you put a plant that's used to experiencing a full 12 hours out in the broiling hot sun on an east-facing sill, you're begging for failure. Your best bet: Choose the sunniest south-facing window available, and if all windows face elsewhere, pick a more forgiving succulent like aloe or throw in the towel and opt for a sturdy pothos.

Not Understanding Their Watering Needs

The Chihuahuan Desert gets a little over 9 inches of rain annually — a drop in the bucket compared to what the verdant landscapes most of us call home receive. In the desert, however, when it rains, it pours. To make your own desert-dweller happy, try to emulate the rainfall patterns native to its home habitat. Don't treat your cacti with a trickle; turn on the taps and let loose a deluge.

All succulents (and all plants for that matter) benefit from a complete soaking, until water comes out of the bottom of the pot. For succulents, wait until the soil is bone dry — and then some — to water again.

Settling for a Standard Potting Soil

Most potted plants come in a standard soil mix that works for almost every kind of plant, from ferns to fiddle-leaf figs. The problem: Succulents are designed to withstand one of the most extreme environments on planet earth, so standard potting soil just won't cut it.

Once you get your succulent baby home, change its soil to a desert-dweller mix, combining half potting soil with something inorganic like perlite. This super well-draining, low-nutrient soil will work for most succulents whether they're used to thriving in the high and dry Andes or the broiling bottom lands of Death Valley.

Overcrowding Them

Succulents tend to come packed into adorable little dishes, all crammed together cheek by jowl. There aren't many plants that like this arrangement, including succulents. Overcrowding is one of the best ways to encourage mold and insect infestations.

The second issue is that, although succulents do very well getting by on slim pickings, they still need food and water. Too much competition means they'll probably miss out. If your succulents arrive in a crowded arrangement, pluck them out carefully and give them each their own spacious mini desert dune.

Growing Impractical Types

I know it's really hard to resist growing saguaros indoors, but please DON'T. Some wild things just aren't meant to be tamed, no matter how pretty their flowers or beguiling their form. Stick instead to the tough little cookies that will happily accept the windowsill as their home sweet home.

Crassula is a good genus to explore if you're working with indoor conditions, as is Sansevieria (a.k.a. snake plant). The Mammillaria cacti (so called for their woolly hair, see above) is another good pick if you're looking for a prickly plant companion.

Advantages of Succulent gardening

Trees and plants perform a crucial role in our lives. Not only for the ecosystem but also for our home they have abundance of advantages.

Among the numerous species of flora present on our planet, succulents are of unique value. Well succulents are those plants which have some or the other part of it fleshy and juicy. This because they are commonly found in arid and dry regions.

So they have to store water in some of their parts for the process of photosynthesis and because of that the part which stores water becomes fleshy. Some succulents store water in their leaves and some in their stems. But each of the succulents has their unique benefits.

The history of succulents goes way back to the pyramid periods. Mr.Rowley author of the book 'History of Succulent Plants' said that these succulents were mentioned in the Egyptian tombs, caves, paintings etc.

The succulents are found in desert and have expanded to the tropical and the subtropical regions. They have also been mentioned in the manuscripts and were considered as the object of art.

Other than objective art pieces succulents can do marvelous wonders in your life.

A Breath Of Fresh Air

benefits of succulents

Just like the smell of the wet soil a breath of fresh air can lighten up your mood in this era of pollution. Succulents take up the carbon dioxide from the atmosphere for the process of photosynthesis and release oxygen as the product of the process. And nothing is better than fresh oxygen which is rare to filter in this polluted environment. In the world where everyone is suffocated in some or the other way succulents act as a source of fresh air.

Adapts To Circumstances

Succulents have the ability to adapt changes very quickly. Coming from the arid regions they are likely to live with extensive sunlight and less water. But when bought to wet and humid climate they adapt themselves to the damp climate circumstances.

Even if there is no sunlight for few days succulents can survive. Storing water has never been an issue for these plants so scarcity of water will also not hamper its growth. For example cactus; they mostly live in the dry regions but when they are planted in humid or indoor climate they adapt to that type of environment.

The Healing Factor

apart from lifting up the mood succulents have the healing factor in them. Some succulents like the stone crops which are leafy succulents have the ability to lower high blood pressure. Just by eating its leaves in the right quantity can lower down the blood pressure.

Other than calming blood pressure succulents can cure sore throat, common cold and dry itchy skin.

Succulents tend to release water which increases the humidity in the atmosphere which cures this disease. A research in University of Kansas has proven that succulents increase the pain tolerance capacity and aid in quick recovery of the patient.

The Strength Of Increasing Concentration

Succulents come in different sizes, colours and shapes. From the thorny ones to ones with bright flowers; they tend to brighten up the room. The upbeat colours of the succulents increase the concentration and helps in focusing on your goals. Students can keep them on their desks which would help in enhancing memory. Succulents release water along with fresh air which clear ups the mind increasing the clarity of thoughts.

Medicinal Properties

There are many succulents which can be eaten and they have marvelous medical properties in them. One of them got highly famous in recent years. Pink dragon fruit with white pulp and little black seeds is tremendously rich in fiber and is low in calories. Also it is rich in proteins, vitamins, iron and calcium. And there are succulents which cannot be eaten but still when applied it does wonders. For example the pulp of aloe when applied to bruises it cures them, also it is very beneficial for the skin problems like acne, hyper pigmentation and dry skin.

Interior Up-Gradation – One Of The Best Benefits Of Succulents

Succulents have wide range of shape, size and colors. In the history they were considered as the objects of art. Similarly succulents add vibrant color to your home and also act as a decorative piece for your interiors. For instance cactus can be wonderful centerpieces.

Highly Affordable

As succulents are available everywhere they are comparatively economical than the other indoor plants.

Easy To Look After

Succulents do not require high amount of sunlight or water so they are very easy to look after. Other plants need constant water and sunlight along with constant care or else they would dry up. But that's not the case with succulents. You can go out of station and not worry about them drying up. You water them once and it can go on for 5 to 6 days.

Stress Free Plantation

These plants are very easy to multiply. We don't need fussy roots or seeds to grow them. They are multiplied through the technique called vegetative propagation. In this method you directly cut the stem or the leaf of the plant and sow it in the mud. They will directly multiply from it. Not only that if you cut a leaf into half the other half of the leaf will still grow. Succulents are easy to handle and fuss free.

A Cool Gift

In this hyperactive generation succulents have proven to be a cool gift. They have benefits which other plants don't have. Apart from having numerous benefits gifting a succulent will add a personal touch to the gift. It will show that you care for the person. Plus gifting a succulent will ensure that your gift is not lost or exchanged or left unattended.

Creative Usage

As they tend to grow in any climate they can be used in highly creative manner. From the showpiece at the coffee houses to the wall hangings, succulents can decorate the place with a very less effort.

Can Be Eaten

If a proper care of succulents is taken they will bear fruits which can be consumed. These fruits are highly rich in calcium, iron, and vitamins like b1, b2, b6 and b12. Also some of them are packed with proteins.

Bye Bye Hangover

Succulents but to be specific cactus contains flavoring and phenolic which are very useful for medicinal purposes. Also they are high in vitamins and calcium which reduce inflammation in the body.

Weight Loss

These plants are highly rich in fiber and have a lot of water content in it. So if you consume less amount of succulents your stomach will still be full. Because of this you would eat less but will not be deprived from the necessary nutrients which are required by the body.

Fights Cancer

It has been observed that cactus leaf bears several antioxidants which ensure that the healthy cells are free from damaged radicals.

The research in 2009 has shown that these leaves are helpful in prevention of breast, prostate, liver and colon cancer.

Disadvantages of Succulent Gardening

The Wrong Succulents

While most succulents will survive for a while indoors, most will not thrive. Succulents that are grown indoors should tolerate low lighting and grow slowly. Some of the easiest succulents to grow indoors include Haworthia fasciata, Sansevieria trifasciata, and Crassula ovata. Many cacti also do well indoors, such as Mammillaria gracilis fragilis. Often the brightly colored succulents seen in arrangements and gardens in the ground will start to turn green, stretch out and lose their shape indoors. However, if you buy a brightly colored arrangement like this it will last much longer than an arrangement of cut flowers and you don't have to take care of it!

Most succulents will stay alive for a couple weeks with little to no care.

No drainage hole

Unless you are extremely careful with how much and how often you water, you'll want your succulents in a pot with a drainage hole. The roots of the succulents will quickly rot if they sit in wet soil for too long. While there is a great selection of pottery with drainage holes, many don't. Either avoid these pots or add a drainage hole by using a diamond tip drill bit. You can add a drainage hole to almost anything!

The Wrong Soil

As mentioned above, succulents will rot and die if they are in wet soil for too long. If you buy your succulents from a big box store like Lowes or Home Depot, they will likely be planted in a very rich soil that retains water and stays wet for a long time. Instead of keeping them in this soil, you'll want to buy a cactus mix which is readily available at these same stores. Another great option for indoor succulent soil is diatomaceous earth. The easiest form of diatomaceous earth to find is Oil-dry, designed to clean up oil spills. Most auto parts stores and many hardware stores will carry this. You can mix this in with a standard potting soil or use it on it's own. diatomaceous earth absorbs water but dries out quickly. This is perfect for succulents. If you find you really like to water plants, using diatomaceous earth as the soil for your succulents will help prevent over watering.

Not enough light

Most succulents need full sun to maintain their color and shape. You'll want to put your succulents in a south facing window where they receive light for most of the day. You may still notice some stretching if you are growing Echeverias which grow quickly and need lots of sunlight. If you grow Haworthias, Gasterias, and Sansevierias however, you'll be able to get by with just a few hours of light per day.

Worrying too much

While succulents do need water to thrive, most will tolerate several days and even a week or two without water before they'll start to shrivel and die. Overwatering is the quickest way to kill your succulents. Generally succulents are inexpensive to buy so take it easy, experiment, and see what succulents do best where you live. Fussing over your succulents will likely result in too much watering and quickly lead them to their death. It's much easier to revive a succulent that has had too little water.

conclusion

Thus with little care we can grow these beautiful plants. when grown indoor a succulent can benefit you in numerous ways from being a decorative piece to lifting up your mood.

From providing vitamins to fighting deadly cancer cells succulents have tremendous qualities. Just imagine what a small plant can give you while you have to invest very less amount of time nurturing it. Succulents are easy to maintain and free of all the fussy procedure.

These little plants can fill your home with vibrant colours and positive energy. Succulents have a great effect on our imagination because of their pretentious nature they appeal to us. Add on benefit of planting succulents in your garden is that it acts as barrier between the garden and the intruder.

The spiny succulents have aggressive- defensive quality which makes them a good protector. Some of the succulents bear flower which are a very pretty sight. The echinocereus reichenbachii cactus is known for its splendid flowers.

From the low mats of ice plants to the flashy sun blooming in the tropical, succulents have it all. Cherry on the cake is all of the benefits at a very affordable price. So go to your nearby nursery and bring back a succulent for you and your loved ones.

Made in United States
Troutdale, OR
09/12/2023